de Havilland
TWIN BOOMS

de Havilland
TWIN BOOMS

Vampire, Venom and Sea Vixen

A D R I A N   B A L C H

Airlife

England

Acknowledgements

This is not intended to be a comprehensive history of these three types, illustrated by copious numbers of black and white photographs that have been published many times before. This is a fresh look at these famous types, for the first time nearly all in colour, with some very rare photographs, most of which have never been published before. It is impossible to produce such a book entirely in colour depicting all three types in operational conditions in the 1950s, so this is a look at the last airworthy examples and the many preserved survivors. Many of the photographs are from my own cameras and some from long-standing very good friends, for which special thanks go to Werner Gysin-Aegerter, Stephen Wolf, Dick Ward, Jeff Peck, Peter Arnold, Steve Hazell, John Stevens and Jerry Shore of the FAA Museum. Wherever possible, the original photographer has been credited where known, but where slides have passed through several hands over the years, please forgive me if someone isn't acknowledged. Thanks also go to the members and staff of de Havilland Aviation Ltd and the Bournemouth Aviation Museum for facilities with G-CVIX.

Copyright © 2002 Adrian Balch

First published in the UK in 2002
by Airlife Publishing Ltd

British Library Cataloguing-in-Publication Data
A catalogue record for this book
is available from the British Library

ISBN 1 84037 250 8

This book contains rare photographs and the publishers have made every endeavour to reproduce them to the highest quality. Some, however, have been technically impossible to reproduce to the standard that we normally demand, but have been included because of their rarity and interest value.

Typeset by Rowland Phototypesetting Ltd, Bury St Edmunds, Suffolk
Printed in China

Airlife Publishing Ltd
101 Longden Road, Shrewsbury, SY3 9EB, England
E-mail: airlife@airlifebooks.com
Website: www.airlifebooks.com

Contents

Introduction

The de Havilland Vampire, Venom and Sea Vixen were all jet fighter aircraft designed and developed in the 1940s and 50s with one thing in common – they all evolved around a twin-boom tail configuration with the engines in the fuselage centre section. Alongside the Gloster Meteor, the Vampire and Venom were the first effective British jet fighters of the post-war period, whose success led to the development of the twin-engined Sea Vixen. Having seen many examples of all these classic fighters in the air and on the ground, I have been impressed by their reliability and gracefulness. The Vampire and Venom were still operated by the Swiss Air Force until the early 1980s and many of these aircraft are still lovingly maintained in airworthy condition today by private individuals worldwide to delight future generations of aviation enthusiasts. Don Wood and his Source Classic Jet Flight at Bournemouth have several airworthy examples of both the Vampire and Venom, repainted to commemorate various milestones in the life of the Vampire and Venom. Alas, although several examples of the larger Sea Vixen are preserved, only one is airworthy today. This is XP924/G-CVIX, which is operated by de Havilland Aviation Ltd at Swansea, South Wales and is at Bournemouth at the time of writing.

The de Havilland Engine Co. Ltd, led by Maj. Frank Halford, started work on the then new jet engine in 1941, after visiting Sir Frank Whittle at Cranwell. Initially called the Halford H 1 engine, it was later renamed 'Goblin'. To avoid loss of performance and assist development, a design with a short jet pipe was required. This resulted in the Vampire with its unusual twin booms and tail configuration, which kept weight and drag to a minimum. When the Goblin was ready for flight testing, the Vampire, although several problems had been overcome, was still not fit to fly,

so the Goblin engine was installed in the Meteor prototype for its maiden flight on 5 March 1943. Six months later, it was the turn of the Vampire, which made its maiden flight from Hatfield on 20 September 1943. This, then, was the start of a successful series of famous de Havilland fighters sharing the 'twin-boom' tail configuration.

The Vampire, Venom and Sea Vixen types have been featured many times in books and articles illustrated with black and white photographs, mainly well-known de Havilland company photographs, but to produce this book entirely in colour has been a challenge, which I'm sure you will appreciate. In many cases, it has not been possible to obtain colour photographs to show the history of these types, as such pictures are virtually non-existent. I did not want to use the same few colour photographs that have been published many times before, but have mainly used previously unpublished views, many of them very rare, thanks to some very good friends around the world. In many countries, photographing military aircraft during the 1960s and 70s was forbidden, and risks were taken to secure some of the photographs in this book. Often, where armed guards didn't know the difference between an aviation enthusiast and a spy, they might shoot first and ask questions later! Many of the photographs in this book were taken under such conditions in order to bring you such rare photographs.

Now, sit back, imagine the unique whining sound of a Goblin or Nene engine, as a Vampire taxies out, or the roar of a pair of Rolls-Royce Avons as a Sea Vixen prepares to launch from a carrier and . . . enjoy!

Adrian M. Balch

The DH 100/113/115 Vampire

De Havilland developed the Goblin engine in late 1941, after Sir Geoffrey de Havilland went to see the pioneering work of Sir Frank Whittle with the Gloster E 28/39. The Vampire was virtually designed around the Goblin engine, with the prototype making a successful first flight from Hatfield on 20 September 1943, in the hands of Sir Geoffrey de Havilland Jnr, son of the company's founder. By the end of the war, the 3100 lb Goblin was the most powerful jet engine in production in Britain. The type entered service with the RAF in 1946 as the Vampire F 1. This was followed by the Vampire F 3, which eventually replaced the Vampire F 1s in RAF service and was the basis for a series of export Vampires, four going to Norway and 85 to Canada. A production line was set-up in Australia and 80 were built by de Havilland Aircraft Pty Ltd, powered by Australian-built Rolls-Royce Nene engines and designated Vampire FB 30. A ground-attack variant of the Vampire F 3, with strengthened wing and reduced span, entered production as the Vampire FB 5 and this attracted a number of export orders. Examples were supplied to Egypt, Finland, France, Iraq, Lebanon, New Zealand, Norway, Sweden and Venezuela. Some standard FB 5s were supplied to the Indian and South African Air Forces and licensed production was negotiated with several countries. In Italy, Macchi built 80 Vampire FB 52As, while Switzerland produced 178 Vampire F 6 aircraft and France 67 Vampire FB 6s. The last of these was assembled from British-made components by SNCASE (Société Nationale de Constructions Aéronautiques Sud Est), who subsequently built 183 Goblin-powered Vampire FB 5s and 250 Vampire FB 53s with French-built Rolls-Royce Nene engines, being designated Sud-Est SE-535 Mistral.

The Royal Navy expressed an early interest in the Vampire for shipboard operations and one of the original prototypes was modified with increased flap area, arrestor hook and long-travel landing gear. The Vampire was the first pure jet aircraft ever to operate from a carrier and was flown aboard HMS *Ocean* by Lt-Cdr E. M. Brown, RNVR, on 3 December 1945. It was followed by two further prototypes and 18 production adaptations of the Vampire 5, re-designated Sea Vampire 20. With a further order, the Fleet Air Arm had a total of 30. A further development of the Sea Vampire was the F 21, of which six were produced by converting F 3s with strengthened bellies for landing trials on flexible rubberised decks without undercarriage.

The last single-seat Vampire variant to serve with the RAF was the FB 9, which was an FB 5 with cockpit air-conditioning. This version served with the air forces of Ceylon (Sri Lanka), Jordan and Rhodesia (Zimbabwe). The latter used both single- and two-seater Vampires for 30 years, right up to at least 1982.

Total UK production of single-seat Vampires exceeded 1900 when the production line closed in December 1953. The Dominican Republic was still using a handful of Vampire FB 50s in the 1980s, but the very last air arm to use the type was the Swiss Air Force, which finally retired its last Vampire FB 6s in 1992.

The DH 113 Vampire NF 10 was a night-fighter development of which 95 were built, mainly for the RAF. Italy had a few delivered, designated Vampire NF 54 and 29 ex-RAF aircraft were sold to the Indian Air Force between 1954 and 1958.

An initial order came from the Egyptian government, who ordered 12 two-seat Vampire night-fighters in October 1949. These aircraft employed an adaptation of the nose from the Mosquito NF 36. However, following the first Arab–Israeli war, arms sales to Egypt were forbidden and the new night-fighters were diverted to the RAF as the DH 113 Vampire NF 10, joining No. 25(F) Squadron at West Malling, Kent, in June 1951. The wide side-by-side seating in the Vampire NF 10 helped develop the DH 115 Vampire Trainer, flown from Christchurch on 15 November 1950 as a private venture with Martin-Baker ejector seats. The success of this version resulted in production orders from the RAF and Royal Navy. The first RAF deliveries were made in 1952, and in 1956, the Vampire T 11 became the standard RAF trainer with the RAF College at Cranwell. The Royal Navy also took delivery of a small number in 1954, with the respective designations being Vampire T 11 and Sea Vampire T 22. More than 530 went to the RAF and 73 to the RN from a total UK production of 804, completed in 1958. Export deliveries as Vampire T 55s went to Austria (5), Burma (8), Ceylon (Sri Lanka) (5), Chile (5), Egypt (12), Eire (6), Finland (5), India (5), Indonesia (8), Iraq (6), Japan (1), Lebanon (3), New Zealand (12), Norway (4), Portugal (2), South Africa (21), Sweden (57), Switzerland (39), Syria (2) and Venezuela (6). Ex-RAF Vampire T 11s were also supplied to Jordan (2) and Rhodesia (Zimbabwe) (4). Additionally, 109 were built in Australia under the designations Vampire T 33, T 34 and T 35, and 50 were assembled in India.

The Vampire T 11 served the RAF well into the 1960s, alongside the Meteor T Mk 7, later aircraft being provided with ejector seats. Worldwide production, including prototypes, reached 4206 aircraft.

The oldest surviving Vampire is F 1, VF301, seen on gate guard duties at Debden on 17 February 1968. It served with No. 226 Operational Conversion Unit (OCU), Nos 595 and 631 Squadrons, then with No. 103 Flying Refresher School, and No. 208 Advanced Flying School, before having a Category 3 accident, which rendered it a non-effective airframe by May 1953. It was then moved to Debden for display and remained there until acquired by the Midland Aircraft Preservation Society in 1973 for £100! (*Photo: Jeff Peck*)

Above: The same aircraft, more than 20 years later, beautifully preserved in the markings of No. 605 Squadron, Royal Auxiliary Air Force in the Midland Air Museum, Coventry on 31 March 1989 coded 'RAL-B'. (*Photo: Adrian Balch*)

Below: VF301 is seen once again, with a slight code change to 'RAL-G', when photographed three years later on 6 August 1992. (*Photo: Adrian Balch*)

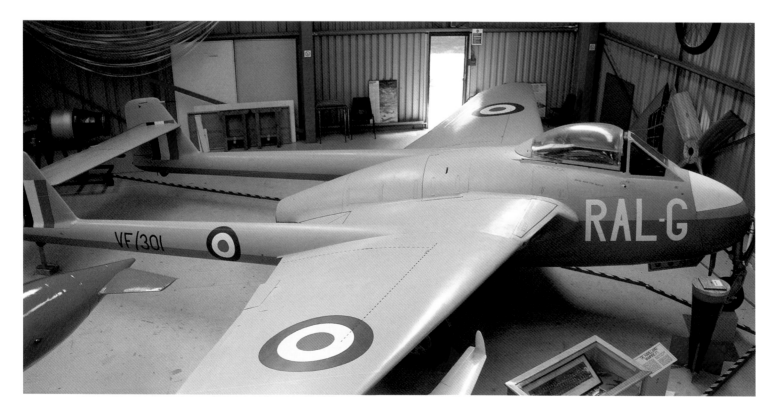

Above: The RAF Museum's FB 3, VT812, in No. 601 Squadron, Royal Auxiliary Air Force markings, which it wore during 1952, seen basking in the sunshine at Abingdon on 14 June 1968, during the RAF's 50th Anniversary celebrations, with a Meteor F 8 of No. 85 Squadron behind. This aircraft was withdrawn from use in 1955 and was stored at Cardington, prior to joining the Colerne collection in 1964. It was moved to Shawbury when Colerne closed in August 1975, then to Cosford the following year, before being installed in the RAF Museum at Hendon, where it can be seen today. (*Photo: Adrian Balch*)

Above: Vampire FB 5, VV542 was preserved by the Air Training Corps (ATC) at Hertford when this photograph was taken on 10 November 1968, but was subsequently scrapped. (*Photo: Stephen Wolf*)

Above: Not a Vampire in a Dracula film! This is Vampire FB 5, VZ304 with a fictitious code 'Z-77' painted black overall for a BBC film, along with a Meteor NF 14 in the same scheme. This Vampire actually served with No. 249 Squadron, RAF, during the early 1950s, but suffered several accidents in service. In February 1960, it was withdrawn from use and placed on gate guardian duties at Carlisle, until 1976, when it was sold to Sandy Topen and moved to Duxford for restoration to static display. It was photographed at Duxford on 23 October 1982. (*Photo: Willie Wilson*)

Above: Last used by No. 3 Civil Anti-aircraft Cooperation Unit (CAACU) at Exeter in 1959, WA450 was a Vampire FB 5 that was nicely preserved by the ATC at Woking at the time it was photographed on 13 April 1968, but has since been allowed to deteriorate and had to be scrapped. (*Photo: Jeff Peck*)

Above: WL505 is a Vampire FB 9 and is seen here as part of the RAF Museum's reserve collection at St Athan on 16 September 1978 in the markings of No. 73 Squadron. It is currently privately owned by de Havilland Aviation at Swansea, registered G-FBIX in anticipation of getting it flying again. (*Photo: Stephen Wolf*)

Above: A moody winter setting, as Vampire T 11, WZ415, of Nos 3/4 CAACUs prepares to depart Exeter on 12 November 1969, for another sortie. (*Photo: Jeff Peck*)

Above: Vampire T 11, WZ458, was part of the Southend Historic Aircraft Collection when it was photographed on 29 March 1969. It was subsequently scrapped, with the nose going to the Blyth Valley Aviation Collection at Walpole, Suffolk. (*Photo: Bob Burgess*)

Above: WZ507 was one of the last Vampire T 11s in RAF service, with the Central Air Traffic Control School (CATCS) at Shawbury. These were the only RAF Vampires to adopt the later light grey and dayglo orange scheme. On retirement in 1970, it went to Carlisle for preservation, but subsequently was made airworthy again by Sandy Topen and his Vintage Aircraft Team at Cranfield, where it was photographed on 10 August 1986, registered G-VTII, accompanied by ex-Swiss Venom FB 54, G-VENI, which was also airworthy. (*Photo: Adrian Balch*)

Above: The same Vampire T 11, WZ507/G-VTII, giving a spirited display at Biggin Hill on 19 June 1988. (*Photo: Adrian Balch*)

Above: Five years later, WZ507/G-VTII is seen here repainted in the markings of Nos 43/151 Squadrons at Cranfield on 19 September 1993. (*Photo: Adrian Balch*)

Above: WZ515 was formerly operated by No. 4 Flying Training School (FTS) at Valley and is seen at Staverton with the Skyframe Aircraft Collection on 14 July 1974. It currently survives with the Solway Aviation Society at Carlisle. (*Photo: Adrian Balch*)

Above: Vampire T 11, WZ584/K, of the Central Air Traffic Control School at Shawbury, photographed at Hatfield on 21 December 1970 in retirement. It is currently preserved with a private collector at Sandtoft, Doncaster. (*Photo: Dick Winfield*)

Left: The Central Air Traffic Control School at Shawbury operated XD382 for many years, so it was appropriate to mount it at the gate. The all-red colour scheme has no significance, apart from its dramatic appearance, effectively displayed in this night shot taken on 3 August 1971. (*Photo: Adrian Balch*)

Right: A few years later, XD382 had been repainted in its correct training colours, when photographed at Shawbury's gate on 6 April 1976. It is currently kept on a pole in a scrap yard at Ripley, Derbyshire. (*Photo: Adrian Balch*)

Below: XD452 last flew with No. 3 FTS, until it made its last flight to Shawbury on 1 September 1967. It was then taken by road to London Colney for preservation by the Mosquito Aircraft Museum at Salisbury Hall, arriving there on 19 February 1968. It is seen there shortly after, on 9 March. (*Photo: Jeff Peck*)

Left: Ten years later, XD452 was mounted on a pole at RAF Cranwell and repainted as 'XD429', one of the RAF College's aircraft during the 1950s. It was photographed at Cranwell on 5 July 1987. However, corrosion and rot set in to the part-wooden airframe and it was broken up, with the nose going to RAF Sealand. (*Photo: Willie Wilson*)

Below: XD506 was last used by the Central Air Traffic Control School at Shawbury, but was retired to the Finningley museum in the mid-1960s. By 1972, it had been repainted in the markings of No. 607 Squadron, Royal Auxiliary Air Force, and moved to Chivenor, where it was photographed on 4 August 1972. It now resides with The Jet Age Museum at Gloucester. (*Photo: Dave Cross*)

Right: A fine shot of Vampire T 11 XD547/Z, of the Central Air Traffic Control School, on finals to Shawbury on 24 April 1968, showing the underwing markings. (*Photo: Jeff Peck*)

Below: A beautiful shot of Vampire T 11 XE860/69, of Nos 3/4 CAACUs at Exeter on 12 November 1969, positively glowing in the autumn sunlight. (*Photo: Jeff Peck*)

Above: Another ex-CATCS Vampire T 11 is XE920, which currently flies with de Havilland Aviation Ltd at Swansea as G-VMPR. It is seen here wearing the markings of No. 603 Squadron, Royal Auxiliary Air Force. This view is particularly useful for showing the topside markings. The aircraft should really be silver, but has been given a light grey paint finish to preserve it more effectively. Adrian Balch took this and all the accompanying close-up detail photographs at Bournemouth on 29 May 2000.
(*Photo: Adrian Balch*)

Right: A close-up of the flaps and air brakes on XE920/G-VMPR.

Above: Nose detail of XE920/G-VMPR.

Right: The cockpit of XE920/G-VMPR is typical of all RAF Vampire T 11s.

The Martin-Baker ejector seats in
Vampire T 11, XE920/G-VMPR.

Right: Vampire T 11, XH304, flew for several years with either Meteor T 7, WF791, or WA669, as 'The Vintage Pair', operated by the Central Flying School (CFS) from Cranwell, until the Vampire collided with WA669 over Mildenhall and both were written-off, on 25 May 1986. The Vampire is seen here performing with WF791 at Biggin Hill on 22 September 1979. Note that both were incorrectly painted light grey, which is a more protective paint than aluminium. Incidentally, Meteor T 7, WF791, also crashed and was destroyed at Coventry on 30 May 1988. (*Photo: Adrian Balch*)

Below: A fine air-to-air study of the late 'Vintage Pair' team of Vampire T 11, XH304, with Meteor T 7 WF791, *circa* 1976 over one of Britain's many white horses, cut out of a chalk hillside. (*Photo: MoD*)

Above: For the very first 'Vintage Pair' team, the Central Flying School used Vampire T 11, XK624 and Meteor T 7, WA669, which are both seen at Little Rissington on 1 August 1970. XK624 survives today with the Norfolk & Suffolk Aviation Museum at Flixton. (*Photo: Adrian Balch*)

Left: The same CFS 'Vintage Pair' team of Vampire T 11, XK624 and Meteor T 7, WA669, showing their underside markings at Little Rissington on 11 September 1971. (*Photo: Adrian Balch*)

Right: An interesting shot of Vampire T 11, XD550, illustrating the solid day-glo paint colour scheme, before dayglo paper strips replaced it. Also, the early CFS coding (which is NOT a Yeovilton code, in case anyone wonders!). This photograph was taken at the Biggin Hill Battle of Britain air display in September 1960. (*Photo: Werner Gysin-Aegerter collection*)

Below: Another example of the early RAF 'solid dayglo' scheme is XE881 of No. 1 FTS, seen at Waterbeach on 15 September 1961, with a No. 64 Squadron Javelin FAW 9R behind. (*Photo: Dick Ward*)

A nostalgic hangar shot 'time capsule' with retired Sea Vampire T 22s and No. 85 Squadron Meteors in storage at Kemble on 16 April 1971, awaiting their fate. Alas, XA128, coded '797/BY', from RNAS Brawdy Station Flight did not survive and was broken up at Kemble shortly afterwards. (*Photo: Adrian Balch*)

Right: Sea Vampire T 22, XA129, did survive with the FAA Museum at Yeovilton and was still in service with HMS *Heron*'s Station Flight at Yeovilton when this photograph was taken at Hatfield on 13 July 1969. (*Photo: Adrian Balch*)

Below: Sea Vampire T 22, XG769, was one of the last in Fleet Air Arm service and was still operated by Lossiemouth's Station Flight when this photograph was taken at Yeovilton on 2 September 1969. (*Photo: Stephen Wolf*)

Left: An earlier shot of XG769 at Yeovilton on 26 June 1964, in the previous overall silver with yellow training bands scheme. Note the stencil-type 'ROYAL NAVY' lettering on the boom. (*Photo: Dick Ward*)

Below: Another glimpse into Kemble's storage hangar on 16 April 1971, with Sea Vampires and Meteors galore! XG772 was one of four operated by RNAS Brawdy's Station Flight and was broken up at Kemble shortly after this photograph was taken (*Photo: Adrian Balch*)

Right: Known as the 'Admiral's Barge', Sea Vampire T 22, XG775, was the personal mount of the Flag Officer, Naval Flying Training at Yeovilton. It is seen there on 9 September 1967. (*Photo: Adrian Balch*)

Below: Another 'Admiral's Barge' was this green and white Sea Vampire T 22, XA160, photographed at Lee-on-Solent on 10 August 1963 (incidentally, the Swordfish behind is NF389, currently being rebuilt to fly). (*Photo: Dick Ward*)

Above: A79-1 was the first Commonwealth Aircraft Corporation (CAC)-built Vampire FB 30 for the Royal Australian Air Force (RAAF) and first flew on 29 June 1949 with a CAC-built Nene engine. The RAAF initially ordered 56 of the type, which were based at Williamtown with No. 2 Operational Training Unit (OTU), where this photograph was taken on 7 April 1973. (*Photo: Gregg Bell*)

Above: Australia has several pole-mounted Vampire FB 30s, including A79-390 at Tamworth, New South Wales. (*Photo: Peter Keating*)

Above: A79-645 heads one of several lines of Royal Australian Air Force Vampire T 35s of the Central Flying School at Pearce, Western Australia, in September 1965. The RAAF ordered 36 Vampire T 33s and 68 T 35s, which had clear-view canopy, ejector seats, increased fuel capacity and dorsal fairings. The final RAAF Vampire sortie was made on 18 September 1970, after which 31 RAAF Vampires had been written off in accidents! (*Photo: Peter Middlebrook*)

Above: Another RAAF Vampire T 35, A79-819, in the markings of No. 2 OCU at Williamtown in May 1968. (*Photo: Author's collection*)

Above: Austria initially operated three ex-Swedish Air Force Vampire single-seat fighters, which were disposed of by 1960. Then they ordered one Vampire T 11 and two T 55s from de Havilland, which were delivered in March 1957. A further five were ordered, which included the last two T 55s built at Chester. A further three ex-RAF T 11s followed. '5C-YC' of the Austrian Air Force was a Vampire T 55, which wears its construction number '15796' underneath the '5C' code. It served with the remainder until April 1972 and is seen here at Linz in October 1966, accompanied by a pair of Austrian Air Force Saab J-29s. (*Photo: Werner Gysin-Aegerter*)

Above: The Royal Canadian Air Force (RCAF) ordered 85 Vampire F 3 fighters from de Havilland in 1946, which were built at Preston and shipped to Canada for reassembly. Two front-line squadrons flew the Vampire, Nos 410 and 421, of which the former formed an aerobatic team called the 'Blue Devils'. This F 3, 17074, is seen preserved with the National Aviation Museum at Rockcliffe, Ottawa in 1967, accompanied by a CF-104G Starfighter, 'Red Knight' T-33 and a P-51D Mustang. (*Photo: Author's collection*)

Right: 17058 is another preserved RCAF Vampire F 3 with the Canadian Museum of Flight and Transportation, Vancouver, British Columbia, where it was photographed on 21 June 1990. (*Photo: Stephen Wolf*)

Above: The Dominican Republic initially bought 25 surplus Swedish Air Force Vampire F 1s (J-28As) in 1955, followed by a further 17 ex-Swedish A.F. J-28B/Vampire FB 50s in 1957. Some of these saw action during the 1959 invasion by Castro-supported revolutionaries and during the 1965 civil war when Vampires attacked rebel positions. The last three were finally withdrawn in October 1974. FAD 2726 and the three aircraft behind it were some of the last in service with the Dominican Air Force when photographed at San Isidro on 20 June 1972. (*Photo: Denis Hughes*)

Above: In 1952, Finland ordered six Vampire FB 52s, followed by four Vampire T 55 trainers in 1955. This order was later increased to nine, including VT-8, which made the last flight by a Finnish Vampire on 15 July 1965 and was afterwards preserved. This photograph was taken at Jyväskylä on 25 June 1977. (*Photo: George Kamp*)

Left: One of the Finnish Air Force's Vampire FB 52s, VA-4 is seen at an unknown location, in operational conditions in the early 1960s, with T 55, VT-1, behind. (*Photo: Werner Gysin-Aegerter collection*)

Above: France ordered 30 Vampire F 1s, which were mostly delivered during 1949. A further 94 ex-RAF Vampire FB 5s were supplied before Sud-Est decided to build a further 67 Vampire FB 51s under licence and 120 FB 51s from parts made in France with the Nene engine built under licence by Hispano-Suiza. The French-built version was known as the Mistral, which was basically a Vampire FB 5 with internal modifications, enlarged air intake to accommodate the Nene and a redesigned fuel system for greater fuel capacity. The first French-assembled FB 51 flew on 27 January 1950. A further 247 were built between June 1953 and February 1954. A pre-production SE-531 Mistral, No. 04, was preserved at La Rochelle when photographed in April 1969. (*Photo: Guido E. Buehlmann*)

Right: The Irish Air Corps initially bought three Vampire T 55s in 1956, followed by another three delivered in 1961. These served faithfully at Casement, Baldonnel, near Dublin, until 1977, when Fouga Magisters replaced them. The very first Vampire T 55 was 185, delivered on 15 May 1956 and seen here at Casement on 10 August 1970. (*Photo: Jeff Peck*)

Left: XE977 was an ex-RAF Vampire T 11 given to the Irish Air Corps in August 1963 for ground instructional training. It retained its RAF serial and is seen here with its engine removed at Casement on 10 August 1970. (*Photo: Jeff Peck*)

Below: The Italian Air Force ordered five Vampire FB 5s, 51 FB 52s and 14 NF 54s off the UK production line, plus 120 FB 52s to be built by Fiat and Aermacchi under licence. The order for 120 FB 52s was later increased to 150, which entered service from 1950 onwards and were all withdrawn from service by 1960. With such a large number, it is surprising that the Italian Air Force Museum had to reconstruct this FB 52A from the parts of MM602, 6014, 6042, 6083 and others. It is seen in the Museo Storico Dell'Aeronautica Militare Italiana at Vigna di Valle on 10 July 1981. (*Photo: Stephen Wolf*)

Right: In 1955, the Japanese Air Self-Defense Force (JASDF) ordered one Vampire T 55 for evaluation, which was delivered in November of that year, with the serial 63-5571. It was demonstrated to JASDF officials the following year, but no orders were placed. This sole aircraft is preserved today and is seen here at Hamamatsu on Christmas Day 1973. (*Photo: Hideki Nagakubo*)

Above: The Lebanese Air Force (LAF) was set up along similar lines to the RAF and was advised to order Vampires, taking delivery of six FB 52s (L152, 153 and L155–158) and three T 55s (L151, 154 and 159) between 1953 and 1955. In addition, the ex-de Havilland T 55 demonstrator (allocated G-APFV), was sold to the LAF in November 1957 as L160. A further seven ex-RAF Vampires were delivered between May and June 1958 to become L161–167. In 1958, the Vampires were used operationally against rebels in the Shouf Mountains and constant air patrols near the Syrian border and Bekaa Valley. This extremely rare shot depicts camouflaged L162 still in service with the Lebanese Air Force, when photographed at Rayak Air Base, Beirut, in August 1966. It is thought to be ex-RAF FB 5, WA128. (*Photo: Werner Gysin-Aegerter collection*)

Left: L166 was another Lebanese Vampire, maintained in better condition than the first one, painted in a smart silver and red scheme, also photographed at Rayak, Beirut, in August 1966 and is thought to be the ex-RAF FB 9, WA365. Most Lebanese Vampires were withdrawn from use in 1964, but these survivors flew until September 1974. (*Photo: Guido E. Buehlmann*)

Below: When the Mexican Air Force began to modernise its fleet in 1960, it bought 15 Lockheed T-33A trainers and 15 Vampire F 3s from Canada. FAM-4 is thought to be ex-RCAF 17017 and was photographed at Santa Lucia in October 1968. It is not thought to be one of the two preserved survivors today. (*Photo: Werner Gysin-Aegerter collection*)

Right: New Zealand ordered 18 Vampire FB 52s as part of a major re-equipment plan for the Royal New Zealand Air Force (RNZAF), which were delivered during 1950/51. Based at Ohakea, No. 14 Squadron was the first to operate the type and another eight were ordered in 1952, followed by a further 21 Vampire FB 5s in 1956 for single-seat training. NZ5776 is seen here at Ohakea in 1970, wearing the markings of No. 14 Squadron and the later 'kiwi' roundels that were changed around that time. This aircraft was previously WA375 with the RAF. (*Photo: Werner Gysin-Aegerter collection*)

Right: The Royal New Zealand Air Force formed an aerobatic team of Vampire FB 5s in 1958 from No. 14 Squadron, which flew at local air shows for three years. They are seen performing at Ohakea on 26 October 1959. (*Photo: RNZAF*)

Right: The second RNZAF Vampire aerobatic team was formed in 1964 by No. 75 Squadron and was known as the 'Yellowhammers', comprising a number of FB 5s and T 11s. Here we see the team with Vampire T 11, NZ5709 at Ohakea in February 1969, their final year. This photograph shows well the old-style RNZAF roundel with silver fern leaf in the centre, flanked by the red and yellow diamond markings of No. 75 Squadron. (*Photo: RNZAF*)

Left: In 1951 an order had been placed by New Zealand for six Vampire T 55s, which were delivered during the second half of 1952, joined by an additional five ex-RAF T 11s in 1955, including NZ5709 which was ex-XH271. It is seen here in No. 75 Squadron markings, still wearing the early fern-leaf-centred roundel at Ohakea on 10 September 1970. The last New Zealand Vampires were finally retired in 1972. (*Photo: John Mounce*)

Above: The Southern Rhodesian Air Force (SRAF) ordered 16 Vampire FB 9s and 16 Vampire T 11s in 1952 to replace its Spitfire 22s. These were ex-RAF and were delivered between 1953 and 1955. With changing politics, the SRAF became the Rhodesian Air Force, then added the 'Royal' prefix to become RRAF. Additional aircraft and spares were supplied by South Africa in 1969, then in 1970 Rhodesia became a republic and the 'Royal' prefix was dropped. The Vampires were then progressively withdrawn and replaced by Hunters, before the country changed its name to Zimbabwe. An anonymous Rhodesian Air Force Vampire T 11 is seen here at Durban on 19 May 1976. The photographer went all over this aircraft to try and find a serial number, or some identification, but in vain! (*Photo: Dave Lawrence*)

Right: The South African Air Force (SAAF) ordered 10 Vampire FB 5s in 1949, which were delivered by sea the following year. A further order for 10 FB 52s and six T 55 trainers was followed by an order for 21 T 55s, all of which were delivered by June 1955. Thirty more Vampire FB 9s were ordered to re-equip No. 2 Squadron, but the majority were withdrawn and scrapped by 1967, with 36 being sold to Rhodesia. A handful remained in service after this time with the last pair of T 55s flying as test beds for electronic equipment at the Test Flight and Development Centre at Waterkloof, being retired in February 1985. SAAF Vampire FB 9, 245 of the Advanced Flying School is seen here at Port Elizabeth on 1 June 1971 with Vampire T 55, 259, in the background. (*Photo: Dave Becker*)

Above: Sweden placed a large order for 70 Vampire F 1s in 1946, which would enter Royal Swedish Air Force service as the J-28A. An even larger order followed for 310 Vampire FB 50s which were designated J-28Bs. All were delivered between 1949 and 1952. In 1953, the RSwedAF ordered 20 of the early model Vampire T 55s and designated them Sk-28Cs. A second batch of 15 updated T 55s followed. The last Swedish Vampires survived until 1968, when they were replaced by Saab 105s (Sk 60s) and the remainder were scrapped or passed to museums. This photograph depicts Vampire T 55/Sk-28C-1, 28425/69, of F-5 Wing at Ljungbyhed in May 1967. This was one of the first batch of early T 55s with framed canopy and no ejector seats. (*Photo: Lars Soldeus*)

Left: In 1949, the *Fuerza Aerea Venezolana* (FAV) ordered 24 Vampire FB 5s to replace its P-47 Thunderbolts. They were delivered by sea in 1952, followed by six Vampire T 55 trainers. All Venezuelan Air Force Vampires were withdrawn from use in 1972, with FB 5, 6035/3C-35, going to the FAV Museum at Maracay, where it is seen on 18 June 1975. (*Photo: Denis Hughes*)

Below: The Venezuelan Air Force Museum at Maracay also houses the FAV's first Vampire T 55, 0023, which was also seen there on 18 June 1975. (*Photo: Denis Hughes*)

Switzerland was the very last country in the world to use the Vampire operationally. The Swiss Air Force was one of the most prolific users, operating the Vampire for 45 years until its official retirement on 12 June 1990. The initial order was for 75 FB 6s in 1948, with a follow-on order for 100 FB 6s the following year, which were to be built under licence by the Federal Aircraft Works (F&W) at Emmen. Vampire T 55 trainers were ordered in several batches totalling twenty, plus 12 Vampire T 11s, of which 9 were ex-RAF, all being modified to T 55 standard. The Vampire FB 6s were modified to operate as fighter-bombers in 1954, when Venoms took over the fighter role. The Vampire fleet was constantly updated and modified, with the single-seaters being relegated to training duties with the arrival of additional Hunters in 1968. In 1971, 55 (plus another four in 1974) of the FB 6 fleet received avionic updates and new UHF radio equipment, which was mounted in a re-profiled nose similar to the Venom. When the type was finally retired from Swiss Air Force service, there were still 59 single-seat and 30 trainers on strength. Many of these were sold to civilian enthusiasts worldwide and have found a new lease of life on the jet warbird scene. J-1101 was the first of the batch of 100 Vampire FB 6s built under licence in Switzerland. It is seen here on finals to Emmen on 28 July 1978. (*Photo: Werner Gysin-Aegerter*)

Left: In 1978 twelve FB 6s were released to join *Zielfliegerkorps* 5 (Aerial Target Corps) for target duties and anti-aircraft units. These aircraft were painted in a spectacular dayglo-red and black striped colour scheme above and below both wing surfaces, with the booms and tail surfaces remaining silver. Vampire FB 6 J-1102, is seen taxiing out at Emmen on 11 March 1981, with a modified 'Pinocchio nose'. (*Photo: Werner Gysin-Aegerter*)

Below: J-1115 was another target-tug Vampire FB 6, this time without the modified Swiss nose, seen at Emmen on 1 May 1980. (*Photo: Werner Gysin-Aegerter*)

Right: Target-tug Swiss Air Force Vampire FB 6, J-1122, is seen in this beautiful air-to-air view near Emmen in October 1989. (*Photo: Author's collection*)

Below: Seen in the twilight of its career, Swiss Air Force Vampire T 55, U-1239, is depicted in the beautiful Alpine winter setting of Samedan on 6 December 1990. (*Photo: Werner Gysin-Aegerter*)

Above: U-1202 was one of two Swiss Air Force Vampire T 55s which were modified in 1968 for trials with AS-11 missiles. It is seen at Sion on 25 November 1981. (*Photo: Werner Gysin-Aegerter*)

Left: The end of the line – literally! The scene at Sion on 23 March 1991, as the last operational Vampires go under the hammer at auction and sale. Most of these Swiss Air Force Vampire T 55s went to warbird owners and museums worldwide. (*Photo: Werner Gysin-Aegerter collection*)

Right: This ex-Swiss Vampire T 55, U-1234, is seen here showing off its de Havilland Goblin 3 engine at Farnborough on 29 July 2000. This aircraft was registered G-DHAV in the hands of de Havilland Aviation Ltd at Swansea. Tragically, it crashed and was destroyed at the Biggin Hill Air Fair on 2 June 2001, killing both occupants. (*Photo: Adrian Balch*)

Below: Another former Swiss Vampire FB 6 was J-1184, which now flies with the Scandinavian Historic Flight as '29683'/SE-DXY and is currently based at North Weald, England. It is seen here in company with former Swiss Air Force Venom FB 50, J-1523, which now flies with the Source Classic Jet Flight, registered G-VENI and is painted as the prototype Venom, 'VV612' (albeit still with the Swiss pointed nose!). The pair were caught together at Coventry on 12 August 2000. (*Photo: Adrian Balch*)

These two ex-Swiss Air Force Vampires are operated by the Source Classic Jet Flight and are (nearest) FB 6, J-1173 (G-DHXX) painted as 'VT871' and T 55 U-1230 (G-DHZZ) painted as 'WZ589'. Both are in RAF No. 54 Squadron markings to commemorate the first jet fighters to fly across the Atlantic, when six Vampire F 3s of No. 54 Squadron flew from Odiham to Goose Bay, via Iceland and Greenland on 14 July 1948. They are seen taking off from Fairford on 24 July 1998. (*Photo: Adrian Balch*)

Another ex-Swiss Vampire T 55 is U-1229, which has found a new home in France as F-AZGO. It is seen here flying in France, in formation with a French Air Force Mirage 2000 of 5 *Escadre* in February 1994. (*Photo: Jean F. Lipka*)

Above: Another ex-Swiss Vampire T 55 was U-1216, which was given to the RAF Benevolent Fund, becoming ZH563. It subsequently joined the Royal Jordanian Air Force Historic Flight and flew as G-BVLM with '209' painted on it. Together with an ex-Swiss Vampire FB 6 and Hunter T 7, these aircraft were operated by Jet Heritage from Bournemouth, where this photograph was taken on 22 August 1995, but are now in Jordan where they fly on special occasions. (*Photo: Adrian Balch*)

Left: Seen here recreating the golden days of the 50s air shows at Wroughton, Wiltshire on 30 August 1993 are the Source Classic Jet Flight with three of their former Swiss Vampire T 55s, U-1230/G-DHZZ, U-1219/G-DHWW and U-1214/G-DHVV, led by former Swiss Venom FB 50, J-1523/G-VENI painted as RAF 'WE402'. (*Photo: Adrian Balch*)

Not what it seems! You could be fooled into believing this shot was taken about 33 years earlier. Is this an 'Admiral's Barge' Sea Vampire with a Meteor NF 11 at Yeovilton photographed in the mid-60s? Actually it was taken at Yeovilton, but on 15 July 2000, and depicts yet another ex-Swiss Vampire T 55, U-1219, which is registered to the Source Classic Jet Flight as G-DHWW, repainted to represent RNAS Yeovilton's 'Admiral's Barge' Sea Vampire T 22, 'XG775', the genuine article of which is illustrated on page 29. (*Photo: Adrian Balch*)

The DH 112 Venom

The de Havilland DH 112 Venom was developed from the Vampire, as a single-seat fighter-bomber powered by a more powerful 5000 lb thrust de Havilland Ghost turbojet. Known initially as the Vampire FB 8, it was redesignated subsequently as a result of extensive changes in the design and was identified easily from its predecessor by its redesigned wing. This had a straight trailing edge instead of the tapered wings of the Vampire, was of thinner section and was equipped to carry jettisonable wingtip fuel tanks.

The first Venom prototype flew from Hatfield on 2 September 1949 and the Venom FB 1 became operational with the RAF just less than three years later, in August 1952. The type saw service in Germany, the Near East and the Far East, equipping 18 squadrons, as well as No. 14 Squadron, Royal New Zealand Air Force. Two-seat Venom NF 2 and NF 3 fighters served between 1953 and 1957 and the Royal Swedish Air Force flew the type until 1960. Overseas, the type was operated by Iraq, Italy and Venezuela.

Following successful manufacture and operation of Vampire FB 6s, Switzerland arranged to build the Venom under licence. Using the same consortium that had produced the Vampire, comprising the Federal Aircraft Factory (EKW) at Emmen, Pilatus at Stans and the Flug und Fahrzeugwerke at Altenrhein, work began in 1953 on a batch of 150 Venom 50s completed to FB 1 standard. A further batch of 100, to FB 4 standard, was completed by 1957. These were designated Venom FB 50 and Venom FB 54 respectively. Of this total of 250, 90 remained in service with the Swiss Air Force by 1981 when they were being retired. During their service, both the Vampires and Venoms were modified by the Swiss to include a redesigned nose housing UHF communications, the strengthening of the inner wing sections to permit the use of rocket-launchers, as well as the introduction of link collectors beneath the cannon.

Royal Navy evaluation of the Venom led to development of a two-seat carrier-based all-weather fighter, the initial production version being designated Sea Venom FAW 20. These had strengthening for catapult take-offs, power-operated folding wings, arrester gear and naval equipment. The type entered service with the Fleet Air Arm in 1954 and also saw service with the Royal Australian Navy and the French Navy.

Four Sea Venom FAW 20 aircraft were assembled in France by Sud-Aviation as the Aquilon 20 and powered by Fiat-built Ghost 48 engines developing 4840 lb (2195 kg) thrust. Licensed production continued with modified undercarriage and other minor alterations being incorporated, resulting in the designations Aquilon 201 (25 built), 202 (25 built), 203 (40 built), with 204 being the French licence-built two-seater trainer, of which a small number were modified from the Aquilon 201s. The first Aquilon first flew from Marignane on 31 October 1952 and production aircraft equipped three *flotilles* with the French *Aéronavale*. The first aircraft were delivered to 16F at Hyères Naval Air Base in early 1955 and some were subsequently detached to Algiers. Aquilons served on board the aircraft carrier *Clemenceau* from 1960 to 1962 until *Flotille* 16F disbanded in 1963. A few Aquilons remained in service until 1965, when an order was received to ground the aircraft. Only one is known to survive, restored by the Musée de L'Air and on display at Rochefort.

There are plenty of former Swiss Air Force Venoms preserved worldwide in museums and maintained in airworthy condition. Unfortunately, there is not one genuine RAF original single-seat Venom preserved in the UK. The last RAF Venom FB 4 was WR539, which was kept outside No. 28 Squadron at Kai Tak, exposed to the Hong Kong humidity for several years until the late 1970s, when it was finally brought back to St Athan for inspection, but found to be so corroded it had to be scrapped. The nose survives with the Mosquito Aircraft Museum and it is currently stored at Staverton, Gloucester. There are just three ex-RAF Venom two-seaters preserved but none airworthy, nor are any Sea Venoms airworthy in the UK, but several of the major UK museums have one. The sole remaining airworthy Sea Venom is currently a former Royal Australian Navy FAW 53 which is privately owned in the USA.

Above: One of only three preserved Venom NF 3 night-fighters is WX853, which is seen here wearing an overall black scheme with its RAF maintenance serial 7443M and RAF No. 23 Squadron markings at Debden. It last flew on 13 April 1957 and moved to Debden for instructional duties on 10 July, where it was photographed on gate guardian duties on 11 November 1967. (*Photo: Dick Winfield*)

Above: The same Venom NF 3, WX853, restored to its correct No. 23 Squadron markings by the Mosquito Aircraft Museum at Salisbury Hall, where it was photographed on 14 August 1971. This Venom saw less than two years' RAF service, being delivered to No. 23 Squadron in October 1955 and being retired in April 1957. It moved from Debden to Salisbury Hall in January 1968. (*Photo: Jeff Peck*)

The Sea Venom was a development of the Venom NF 2, the main difference being a 'V'-shaped arrestor hook mounted in a fairing above the jet orifice. Following carrier trials in July 1951, some refinements were made and the first of 50 production Sea Venom FAW 20s flew on 27 March 1953. In service, the type was found to have weaknesses with the undercarriage and arrestor hook during carrier-based operations and on 12 September 1955, all Sea Venoms were relegated to second-line land-based operations at Yeovilton, with No. 890 Squadron being renumbered 766 for aircrew training. An uprated Ghost 104 engine, powered ailerons and improved radar resulted in the Sea Venom FAW 21. This also had strengthened undercarriage and a raised pilot's seat to give a better view, combined with a modified canopy. The FAW 22 derived from an even more powerful Ghost 105 engine, but with no external changes. The modified and upgraded Sea Venoms returned to carrier operations with Nos. 809, 890, 891 and 892 Squadrons on board HMS *Ark Royal*, *Albion* and *Eagle* in 1955. All three squadrons were involved in the Suez War in 1956. Thirty-nine Sea Venom FAW 22s were built and a number of FAW 21s received the increased power Ghost 105 engine. Sea Venoms were finally retired from front-line duties in 1960 and were relegated to land-based training duties. The last Fleet Arm Unit to operate the type was the Airwork-managed Air Direction School at Yeovilton, which was civilian-manned and operated about a dozen aircraft for radar tracking and air traffic control training. WW138 was one of the Sea Venom FAW 21s operated by this unit and was retired at the end of 1969 and transferred to the Fleet Air Arm Museum. Initially, it was repainted in the colours of No. 809 Squadron, when based aboard HMS *Albion* in 1955 and is seen here at Yeovilton on 11 March 1970. (*Photo: Adrian Balch*)

Left: Here is WW138 twenty-three years later, repainted in No. 809 Squadron's 1956 Suez markings at Yeovilton on 17 July 1993, prior to being installed in the FAA Museum's Carrier Exhibition. (*Photo: Adrian Balch*)

Below: WW151 was one of handful of Sea Venom FAW 21s operated by No. 750 Squadron, which was the Naval Photography and Observers School at RNAS Lossiemouth. It is seen there on 12 May 1970, just prior to its withdrawal. (*Photo: Dave Lawrence*)

Above: One of the Fleet Requirements Unit's Air Direction School Sea Venom FAW 21s was WW217, seen here taxiing in following another sortie at a very wet Yeovilton on 11 March 1970. (*Photo: Adrian Balch*)

Left: Sea Venom FAW 22, XG697, of the Air Direction School is seen getting airborne from RNAS Yeovilton on 9 September 1967, during the annual Air Day. (*Photo: Brian Stainer/APN*)

Left: 'Witchcraft' was the name of No. 890 Squadron's aerobatic team of three Sea Venom FAW 21s, led by WW217 coded '351', seen here in neat formation operating from HMS *Ark Royal* in June 1956. (*Photo: FAA Museum*)

Above: More than thirty years later, we see Sea Venom FAW 21, WW217 (the lead aircraft of the trio) still surviving, beautifully preserved in No. 890 Squadron's markings, in the caring hands of the Newark Air Museum, where it was photographed on 16 May 1988. (*Photo: Adrian Balch*)

Left: 'Hook down and three greens' – finals to a carrier? With a little imagination, perhaps, but this is Sea Venom FAW 21, WW286, of the Yeovilton-based Air Direction School seen during a slow flypast demonstration at Hatfield's Families Day on 5 July 1969. (*Photo: Adrian Balch*)

Below: This Sea Venom FAW 21, XG616, is seen in the markings of No. 766 Squadron with Yeovilton's 'VL' tail code. It was photographed when withdrawn from use at Lee-on-Solent in June 1967. (*Photo: V. E. Gibb*)

Above: The Royal Australian Navy ordered 39 Sea Venoms, which were delivered in March 1955 with the designation FAW 53, which was the export variant of the FAW 21. Their shore base was Nowra NAS, New South Wales, where Nos 805 and 808 Squadrons formed and deployed aboard HMAS *Melbourne* in August 1958. The Australian training squadron was No. 724 which operated the last airworthy Sea Venoms until withdrawal in 1973, some of which were target-tugs. WZ944 was one of these, which retained its British serial number and is seen here at Nowra NAS on 12 October 1969. This is the only Sea Venom still airworthy today and flies in the USA in No. 809 Squadron, Royal Navy markings with Suez stripes, and registered N.7022H. (*Photo: Gregg Bell*)

Right: Seen in a more conventional colour scheme and with Australian serial, is Sea Venom FAW 53, N4.904, also of No. 724 Squadron, Royal Australian Navy at Nowra NAS on 12 October 1969. (*Photo: Gregg Bell*)

Left: This Australian Sea Venom, FAW 53, WZ895, was operated by the Royal Australian Navy Historic Flight from Nowra NAS, and was airworthy when it was photographed on 29 September 1984. (*Photo: via John Hughes*)

Above: In France, the Sea Venom was manufactured under licence by SNCASE at Marignane, Marseilles, powered by an Italian-built version of the Ghost 48/1. Originally designated the Sea Venom FAW 52 by de Havilland, the French renamed it the Aquilon. The prototype flew on 31 October 1952, followed by four pre-production machines. The French variant differed in having French ejector seats, French electronic equipment and an unstressed undercarriage which was designed for carrier landings. The *Aéronavale* took delivery of 25 Aquilon 20s, followed by a further 25 202s, of which the first flew on 24 March 1954. The latter version was intended for carrier operations, having a sliding instead of hinged canopy to permit take-offs and landings with the hood partly open. The stressed under-carriage for carrier deck landings and an improved radar were also features of this variant. A single-seat variant was also developed, designated the 203, with an elongated radar nose and guidance system for the Nord 5103 air-to-air missile. Some 40 were produced. The final variant was the 204, of which 15 were built as dual-seat land-based operational trainers, which carried the standard 20 mm cannon pack for weapons training. Operationally, the Aquilon equipped *Flotille* 16F, which formed at Hyères on 3 February 1955. This was followed by *Flotille* 11F, which joined the newly built aircraft carrier *Clemenceau* in March 1960. *Flotille* 16F joined it also until 11F disbanded on 4 April 1962, leaving 16F to operate some 18 Aquilons between the carriers, *Foch* and *Clemenceau*. Withdrawal of Aquilons from carrier use began in 1964. The last Aquilon flight was made from Hyères on 8 March 1965. French Navy Aquilon 202, No. 45, of *Flotille* 16F is seen coming in to land at Hyères in August 1961. (*Photo: Werner Gysin-Aegerter*)

Right: Aquilon 204 (note the sliding canopy), No. 95 of 59 *Escadrille de Servitude*, the all-weather fighter pilot's school at Hyères in August 1961.

Right: This interesting view of Aquilon 202, No. 64, has its wings folded and nose open to reveal the radar antennas.

Right: This Aquilon 20 was No. 13, from the initial batch of land-based machines with hinged canopy and operated with the *Aéronavale*'s *Esc*.10.*S*.2, which was a training squadron, denoted by liberal amounts of orange dayglo paint. It is depicted at Hyères in August 1961. (*Photos: Werner Gysin-Aegerter*)

Left: An unidentified *Aéronavale* Aquilon 20 from *Esc.*10.*S.*3 showing the underside markings and colour scheme to advantage as it overflies Hyères in August 1961. (*Photo: Werner Gysin-Aegerter*)

Below: A sad end – one month after the last flight, French Navy Aquilon 204, No. 96, is dumped at Hyères in April 1965, together with all the others, their Ghost engines ripped out and scattered alongside! (*Photo: Guido E. Buehlmann*)

Right: When No. 14 Squadron, Royal New Zealand Air Force, moved from Cyprus to Tengah, Singapore, in April 1955, they hired some RAF Venom FB 1s to consolidate the Australian, British and New Zealand forces to tackle the Malayan Emergency and flew alongside the Venoms of the RAF's No. 60 Squadron. Before they left Singapore, No. 14 Squadron, RNZAF formed an aerobatic team with four Venom FB 1s, seen here during 1958 in a neat line-abreast formation. (*Photo: RNZAF*)

Above: The only overseas order for the Venom night-fighter was from the Royal Swedish Air Force, which ordered 62 designated NF 51 (J-33 in Swedish service). The aircraft were all built at Chester, with licence-built Ghost engines supplied by Svenska Flygmotor and shipped to England for installation. These were delivered to F 1 Wing at Vasteras, which served until 1960, when they were all withdrawn from use, apart from four, which were retained and transferred to the civilian company, Swedair of Vidsel, for use as high speed target-tugs on behalf of the Swedish government. Registered SE-DCA to SE-DCD, they were painted in a high visibility scheme of yellow overall. Still carrying its military serial, 33025, SE-DCD is one of the four Venom NF 51 (J-33) target-tug aircraft and is seen here preserved at Malmslätt on 28 August 1976. (*Photo: Willie Wilson*)

Switzerland was the last military operator of the Venom as well as the Vampire. The Swiss Air Force found the Venom ideal for its geographical conditions and commenced licence-building the type in 1953, with 126 FB 1s (J-1501 to J-1625) as FB 50s at F&W, Emmen, Doflug, Altenshein and Pilatus AG, Stans. It also decided that the Ghost 48 engine would be licence-built in Switzerland by Sulzer Brothers at Winterthur. However, the first 35 engines were supplied direct by de Havilland and Swiss-built Ghosts were installed in the 30th aircraft onwards. Because the Swiss government couldn't decide on a replacement, the Swiss Venoms had to remain in service much longer than anticipated and had to have strengthening modifications carried out by F&W at Emmen to combat fatigue in the metal parts, which more than doubled the service life of the aircraft. In 1956, the same group of companies produced 24 reconnais-

sance versions of the Venom FB 1, with serials starting with J-1626. These were known as FB 1Rs, and had underwing tanks fitted with a number of automatic aerial cameras installed in the forward portion. A further production run began in 1956, totalling 100 Venom FB 4s (FB 54s in Swiss service) equipped with UHF radio and an improved bomb-sight. The serial numbers of this variant started with J-1701. The Swiss Air Force Venoms were mainly used in the ground attack role. Around 1970, the Venoms received modifications and updating included new avionics and radar, installed in a reprofiled pointed nose. By the early 1970s, some 200 Venoms were still in service with 14 squadrons, with the final aircraft being withdrawn in the latter half of 1983. Many were transferred to museums and several were sold to enthusiasts, who maintain them in air-worthy condition, mainly in the UK and the USA.

A pair of silver Swiss Air Force Venom FB 50s, led by J-1584, return to Dubendorf after another sortie in June 1968. (*Photo: Guido E. Buehlmann*)

Right: A Swiss Air Force Venom FB 50, J-1641, seen at Emmen in April 1966 in original configuration with the under-wing fuel tanks/recce pods. (*Photo: Werner Gysin-Aegerter*)

Below: A pair of Swiss Venom FB 50s, J-1523 and J-1601, on finals to Dubendorf on 27 August 1983 displaying the modified Swiss 'Pinocchio' nose. (*Photo: Werner Gysin-Aegerter*)

Above: With a crack of the starting cartridge and a plume of black smoke, Swiss Air Force Venoms and Vampires come to life as they start their Ghost and Goblin engines in this wonderful flight-line view at Emmen on 25 May 1981. (*Photo: Werner Gysin-Aegerter*)

Left: A fine landing shot of Swiss Air Force Venom FB 50, J-1641, of No. 10 Squadron with revised 'Pinocchio' nose and underwing fuel tanks/camera pods at Emmen on 25 August 1981. (*Photo: Werner Gysin-Aegerter*)

Above: Non-standard paint schemes on Swiss Venoms were rare. This FB 54, J-1741, was known as 'Lindi's Phoenix 1' and is seen at Ulrichen on 15 September 1978. (*Photo: Werner Gysin-Aegerter collection*)

Right: When the Swiss Venoms retired in 1983, several came to the UK in the hands of civilian enthusiasts. One of the first was this FB 54, J-1790, which had its nose restored to its original shape and was registered G-BLKA to Sandy Topen and the Vintage Aircraft Team at Cranfield. It was repainted as RAF Venom FB 4, 'WR410', of No. 6 Squadron, with Suez stripes and appeared on the UK air show circuit during the late 1980s and early 90s. It is seen here taxiing at Abingdon on 15 September 1990. (*Photo: Adrian Balch*)

Above: Another former Swiss Venom in the UK is this FB 50, J-1539, which became G-DHUU and is also painted as 'WR410' of No. 6 Squadron, but in an RAF desert camouflage. It is a pity that it retains the Swiss pointed nose, which spoils the illusion! This is one of several operated by Don Wood's Source Classic Jet Flight from Bournemouth and is seen at Fairford on 26 July 1998. (*Photo: Adrian Balch*)

Left: Another view of former Swiss Venom FB 50, 'WR410' (G-DHUU) in No. 6 Squadron, RAF markings at Biggin Hill on 15 September 1997. (*Photo: Adrian Balch*)

The Source Classic Jet Flight have repainted their fleet of Vampires and Venoms to represent milestones in the types' careers. This former Swiss Venom FB 50, J-1611, is now registered G-DHTT and marked as 'WR421' to commemorate 50 Years of Jet Display Teams 1947–97. It is painted in Red Arrows red and represents the first jet aerobatic team of Vampires of No. 54 Squadron. This aircraft is seen displayed at Farnborough on 11 September 1998, during the show's 50th Anniversary. (*Photos: Adrian Balch*)

Left: This is one of the Swiss Venom FB 54s that was sold to an enthusiast in the USA. It was formerly J-1730 and now flies at N402DM in a black and orange pseudo-RAF colour scheme. It is seen here at Oceana NAS, Virginia, on 20 April 1986. (*Photo: Stephen Wolf*)

Below: Former Swiss Venoms ended up all over the world, as far away as New Zealand, where FB 54, J-1799, was registered ZK-VNM and beautifully restored to represent an RNZAF Venom FB 1 of No. 14 Squadron. It is seen here at Ardmore on 4 March 1990. (*Photo: John Mounce*)

Right: Exactly five years later, the owner seems to have switched allegiance, reattached the ugly Swiss pointed nose and repainted ZK-VNM in a red and white colour scheme with its original Swiss Air Force serial, J-1799. Perhaps he felt it never was a New Zealand Venom and should be displayed with the only serial it has ever worn! It is seen at Ardmore on 4 March 1995. (*Photo: John Mounce*)

Below: Venezuela ordered 22 Venom FB 54s in July 1955, all of which were built at Chester. The first aircraft was 1A-34, which was delivered to No. 34 Squadron at Maiquetía on 1 December 1955, with the rest following up until 17 August 1956. They remained in service with the Venezuelan Air Force until the end of 1965. 1A-34 is preserved at the FAV Museum at Maracay, where it is seen in September 1968. (*Photo: Author's collection*)

The DH 110 Sea Vixen

Originally designed as a land-based all-weather fighter for the Royal Air Force, in competition with the Gloster Javelin, the prototype de Havilland DH 110 first flew on 26 September 1951. A second aircraft joined this on 26 September 1952, which undertook 'touch and go' trials on HMS *Albion* in the autumn of 1954. The Sea Vixen was built at de Havilland's Christchurch factory, near Bournemouth, as well as at Chester and was powered by two 11 230 lb (5094 kg) thrust Rolls-Royce Avon 208 turbojets. The DH 110 Mk 20X, a partially navalised prototype, first flew from Christchurch on 20 June 1955 and made the first full-stop arrested landing on 5 April 1956 aboard HMS *Ark Royal*. The first of the initial production order for 45 Sea Vixen FAW 1 aircraft introduced a hinged and pointed radome, power-folding wings and a hydraulically steerable nosewheel. This aircraft first flew on 20 March 1957. The type entered service with No. 700Y Flight in November 1958, aboard HMS *Victorious* and HMS *Centaur*. It became operational with No. 892 Squadron at Yeovilton on 2 July 1959 and went to sea in HMS *Ark Royal* in March 1960. Armament comprised four Firestreak air-to-air missiles and two retractable nose pods each with 14.2 in (360mm) rocket projectiles, plus four 500 lb (227 kg) bombs on underwing racks. A total of 114 Sea Vixen FAW 1s were built at Christchurch and Chester.

All aspects of the aircraft underwent trials and development, with XJ476 being allocated to radar and sighting trials at the A&AEE Boscombe Down, before being painted white overall for guided weapons trials on the Woomera ranges in Australia and shipped out with XJ481 on 13 March 1960 for three years. XJ476 went on to develop the Red Top guided missile. XJ477 was also used for armament trials at the A&AEE in early 1960 and undertook carrier trials on HMS *Centaur* the previous year. XJ478 was used for Firestreak development work, with both later joining No. 766 Squadron at Yeovilton. Among the other development and trials machines was XJ481, which was probably the most converted Sea Vixen of all. This machine undertook carrier trials on HMS *Centaur* in 1959, as well as FAA handling trials. It then went out to Woomera for three years and returned to undertake missile development work in 1963, progressing to TV trials during the following two years, operating from Hatfield. These latter trials involved having the usual nose radome replaced by a nose cone fitted with an optically flat glass panel at the front, protecting the TV camera. In November 1968, the aircraft was delivered to A&AEE Boscombe Down and remained there, mainly involved in Martel missile trials, until retired to the Fleet Air Arm Museum at Yeovilton in 1974. It has since been moved to Royal Naval Aircraft Yard (RNAY) Fleetlands.

Cold weather trials were undertaken by XJ482 in the climatic chamber at Weybridge in July 1959 and it became the first aircraft delivered to No. 700Y Flight for service trials at Yeovilton on 3 November 1958.

Other trials included 'buddy' refuelling trials, involving XJ488 and XJ516, bombing and sighting trials, the low altitude bombing system (LABS) technique and Bullpup missile development.

On successful completion of all these intensive service trials, No. 700Y Flight had used a total of eight Sea Vixen 1s. The unit was re-formed and commissioned on 2 July 1959 as No. 892 Squadron, which embarked in HMS *Ark Royal* on 3 March 1960 for sea trials and transferred to HMS *Victorious* later in the year. The squadron then transferred to HMS *Hermes*, before joining HMS *Centaur* in December 1963.

By September 1960, No. 766 Squadron had received its full quota of Sea Vixen 1s as the operational and conversion training unit at Yeovilton. In 1962, instructors from No. 766 Squadron formed an aerobatic team of Sea Vixens at Yeovilton called 'Fred's Five', which took part in the 50th Anniversary of Military Aviation air display at Upavon, as well as at Farnborough and other shows.

On 1 February 1960, No. 890 Squadron was commissioned at Yeovilton, commanded by Lt-Cdr W. H. Hart and joined HMS *Hermes* five months later, then transferred to HMS *Ark Royal*. This was followed by No. 893 Squadron, which commissioned on 9 September 1960. Number 899 Squadron was commissioned at Yeovilton on 1 February 1961 as the Headquarters Squadron to evaluate new operational ideas and maintain the standards of the service units.

At this time, de Havilland was investigating a number of improvements and developments of the basic aircraft, including replacing the Avon engines with 11 380 lb thrust Rolls-Royce Spey engines. Also, fitting additional 250 gal wingtip fuel tanks, plus an 850 gal fuel tank behind the cockpit in a lengthened fuselage. An easier solution resulted in additional pinion fuel tanks added ahead of the tail booms.

The Red Top air-to-air missile was to replace the Firestreak, and other refinements resulted in the Sea Vixen FAW 2. Initially, two development aircraft, XN684 and 685 were converted from Mk 1s and were flown on 1 June and 17 August 1962 respectively, both later being brought up to full Sea Vixen FAW 2 standard at Chester. Following trials at A&AEE Boscombe Down, they joined No. 893 Squadron on HMS *Hermes* in 1968. Fourteen Mk 1s were completed as Mk 2s on the line, the first flying on 8 March 1963. This was followed by 15 new-build Mk 2s and a further 67 conversions from Mk 1s. The Sea Vixen FAW 2 entered service with No. 899 Squadron at Yeovilton in December 1963, which embarked in HMS *Eagle* a year later. It is noteworthy that No. 899 Squadron was part of HMS *Eagle*'s air group when she was finally decommissioned in 1972. XN684 eventually made the final Sea Vixen deck landing while serving with No. 899 Squadron on HMS *Eagle*, before returning to Yeovilton on 23 January 1972 to decommission and was scrapped at Sydenham the following year, along with a number of others.

The first production Sea Vixen FAW 2 was XP919, which first flew from Chester on 8 March 1963, and in addition to the new-build aircraft, most of the surviving Mk 1s were converted to Mk 2 standard at Chester and Sydenham. Following trials at Boscombe Down, XP919 joined No. 766 Squadron in 1968 until being transferred to No. 890 Squadron in 1971, both at Yeovilton.

Number 899 introduced the new version of the Sea Vixen into service, as it was the Yeovilton-based headquarters squadron. The Squadron embarked in HMS *Eagle* in December 1964 and participated in the Rhodesian blockade, until returning to Yeovilton in August 1966. Number 766 Squadron received its first Mk 2, XS582, on 7 July 1965, while No. 893 Squadron began re-equipping on 4 November 1965. Number 890 Squadron disbanded briefly in 1966, but was recommissioned as the new headquarters squadron in September the following year with Mk 1 and 2 Sea Vixens. Number 892 Squadron re-equipped with the Mk 2 in 1963, joining HMS *Hermes* in time to participate in the Aden crisis. When they returned to Yeovilton in February 1968, No. 892 Squadron formed the second FAA Sea Vixen aerobatic team, 'Simon's Sircus', with six aircraft led by Lt-Cdr Simon Idiens. This lasted just for one season, taking in air shows at Yeovilton and Farnborough, the aircraft being equipped to make blue smoke. At the end of the season, No. 892 Squadron disbanded in October 1968 to mark the start of the Sea Vixen's retirement from service, making way for entry into service of the Phantom FG 1 the following April. When HMS *Hermes* returned to Portsmouth in July 1970, No. 893 Squadron also disbanded and most of its Sea Vixens were flown to Sydenham, Belfast, to be scrapped between 1971 and 1973. Number 766 Squadron followed, being disbanded at Yeovilton on 10 December 1970. The training task was passed to No. 890 Squadron, who in turn, finally disbanded on 6 August 1971 and passed the training over to the Airwork-operated Fleet Requirements Unit (FRU) at Yeovilton, which was the last land-based FAA Sea Vixen unit. Number 899 Squadron was the last shipborne unit, which remained on HMS *Eagle* until returning to Yeovilton and finally disbanding on 23 January 1972. Five of its aircraft were delivered to Llanbedr for evaluation as drones and others went to Farnborough for drone conversion. The aircraft had all their unwanted equipment removed at Farnborough and were ferried to Tarrant Rushton for conversion to U 3 drones by Flight Refuelling.

As funding for this programme was short, only a handful of conversions were completed and work petered out, with just XJ524, XP924, XS577 and XS587 taking to the air in FAW (TT) 2 form, which was shortly redesignated D 3. Of these four, all wore different variations of the drone colour scheme and had limited service at Llanbedr, being retired to Hurn and disposal.

The FRU Sea Vixens remained in service at Yeovilton until they were also withdrawn in January 1974. This left just two Sea Vixens flying; XJ572 with the Sydenham Station Flight as a hack and XN653 with the Royal Aircraft Establishment at Bedford and both were due for retirement.

. . . And then there was one

As this is written, there are some sixteen Sea Vixen survivors throughout the UK and one in Australia, in varying conditions, with museums and private enthusiasts, plus a further eleven nose sections in museums and collections, which shows the level of importance enthusiasts put on the type and the robust construction of an aircraft designed for operating in a harsh environment. Of the four retired drones, XJ524 was taken to Catterick by road in 1984 for fire training and XS577 was scrapped at Hurn in 1984 with the nose section going to an enthusiast in Switzerland. XS587 was put on the civil register as G-VIXN in anticipation of it flying in civilian hands with Jet Heritage at Bournemouth, but costs and problems with civilian certification were too great and the aircraft was sold to a private collector at Charlwood, near Gatwick, where it can be seen today on static display.

So we come to the final airworthy Sea Vixen, D 3, XP924, which survives airworthy to this day thanks to the efforts of former Sea Vixen pilot Marcus Edwards and his team led by Gwyn and Gary Jones. Against all odds, this aircraft got CAA certification on the civil register as G-CVIX on 26 February 1996.

Following service with No. 899 Squadron, XP924 was ferried to RAE Llanbedr, where it was stored until February 1975, prior to joining the drone conversion programme at RAE Farnborough. Over the next 10 years, it flew a total of only 31 hours and was fully converted to Sea Vixen D 3 drone standard by 10 June 1985. It was delivered to Llanbedr for service on 6 January 1986 but flew little, making its final flight on 24 January 1991.

When XP924 was retired at Llanbedr in January 1991, a new aircraft enthusiast group, including Gwyn and Gary Jones was set up at Swansea Airport, called de Havilland Aviation Ltd. Marcus Edwards became Chief Pilot. The Sea Vixen was offered for sale by tender in November 1995, together with the other two Sea Vixen drones, and was purchased by Gwyn's wife, Jacqui, the managing director, in January 1996, together with a substantial stores package of some 2300 items, including five Rolls-Royce Avon 208 turbojets. The team got the CAA involved and slowly and carefully brought XP924 back up to full flying standard. Monthly engine and taxi runs were carried out and the CAA permitted the aircraft to be flown from Llanbedr to Swansea on 2 August 1996, piloted by former German *Luftwaffe* Starfighter pilot, Sepp Pauli, now Chief Test Pilot of Defence Test and Evaluation Organisation (DTEO) Llanbedr, and Marcus Edwards. With several 'technical snags' *en route*, the Sea Vixen made it safely to Swansea. There, work began in earnest to get it up to full CAA display standard in the hope of displaying it during the 1997 air show season. XP924 flew 800 of its total 1140 hours flying time with No. 899 Squadron, much of it aboard HMS *Eagle* and Marcus Edwards had flown it 24 times between January 1965 and July 1970, so it is hoped that it will be repainted with No. 899 Squadron's white winged-fist insignia. The team had several setbacks, not least was the untimely death of Marcus Edwards, who would never see his dream fulfilled. However, in his honour, his wife pledged that the project should continue with the support of Gwyn Jones and the team, who continued to work on the last airworthy Sea Vixen. Solving technical problems and completing all the CAA paperwork was no mean feat, but they were determined to see her fly again. Finally, on Bank Holiday Monday 29 May 2000, XP924/C-CVIX took to the air once again, this time piloted by Sepp Pauli and Clive Rustin, with a CAA Permit to Ferry for the aircraft to fly to Bournemouth–Hurn for more attention by the engineers at the Bournemouth Air Museum. The year 2000 was the 50th Anniversary of the Farnborough Air Show and it was hoped that the Sea Vixen would make the celebrations, but alas it was dogged by more CAA paperwork and didn't make it. G-CVIX was finally cleared for display flying and made a 35 minute test flight on 16 February 2001, piloted by CAA test pilot Dan Griffith. Now the world could once again see a Sea Vixen fly!

What a way to treat a prototype! The sole DH 110 Mk 20X all-weather fighter prototype, XF828 is seen here being used for fire practice at RNAS Culdrose on 15 October 1970, shortly before it was scrapped! Obviously its historical significance was not recognised and they thought this was just *another* 'Sea-Vixen'. XF828 made its maiden flight on 20 June 1955 piloted by Jock Elliott and powered by a pair of uprated Avon 208s. It did not have folding wings, but was otherwise designed for flight deck operations. Trials began from Hurn in 1956 and full sea trials were carried out aboard HMS *Ark Royal*. This was the first of its type to carry out an arrested landing and catapult launch, on 5 April 1956, piloted by Lt-Cdr S. Orr. Following these trials, XF828 was passed to the Royal Aircraft Establishment for further trials utilising Bedford's dummy flight deck facilities until 28 November 1960, when it left to become a ground instructional airframe at RNAS Culdrose. (*Photo: Jeff Peck*)

Right: XJ476 was an early Sea Vixen FAW 1 that was originally allocated to radar and sighting trials at the A&AEE. It was then painted white for guided weapons trials at Woomera in Australia and shipped out on 13 March 1960, together with XJ481. Both aircraft returned to Hatfield in March 1963 and XJ476 resumed guided weapons trials with Hawker Siddeley Dynamics, mainly as a radar target for Red Top development. It was then used in the Martel missile programme at A&AEE Boscombe Down until it was retired in 1973. It was then scrapped, but the nose section survives in the Southampton Hall of Aviation. It is seen at Boscombe Down on 18 March 1971. (*Photo: Adrian Balch*)

Above: Another trials aircraft was this all-black FAW 1, XJ488, which was initially used for flight refuelling trials using the 'buddy' technique of carrying its own flight-refuelling pod under the wing instead of the usual fuel tank. It was then used for systems and weapons development for many years, including engine performance, LOX (liquid oxygen) trials and radar during 1962. In November 1963, it began Red Top computer trials at Hatfield. Then further weapons trials involving Bullpup and LABS (low altitude bombing system) development began in January 1965 at Bedford, then at Boscombe Down. It joined 'C' Squadron at the A&AEE on 18 October 1967 and was painted in this overall black scheme in 1968. It was finally relegated to fire practice at Boscombe Down in 1973, but the nose was saved and is with the Robertsbridge Aviation Society at Mayfield. It is seen on finals to Boscombe Down on 6 June 1970. (*Photo: Adrian Balch*)

This odd-looking Sea Vixen FAW 1 is XJ481, which has had a very eventful history. It first carried out carrier trials aboard HMS *Centaur* in 1959, as well as FAA handling trials. It was then shipped out to Australia in March 1960 for guided weapons trials on the Woomera ranges, together with XJ476. On its return from Australia in March 1963, it was based at Hatfield and used for missile development trials, followed by TV trials. For these, the usual pointed nose radome was fitted with an optically flat glass panel, behind which a camera was installed. From November 1968, trials continued at Boscombe Down involving the Martel missile programme. The unusual black and white colour scheme is split diagonally across the aircraft! The aircraft remained there until it was retired to the Fleet Air Arm Museum at Yeovilton in 1974. It was later transferred to Fleetlands, where it resides today. XJ481 is seen here on approach to Boscombe Down on 13 July 1970. (*Photo: Adrian Balch*)

Right: An interesting detail shot of XJ481 on arrival at the Fleet Air Arm Museum at Yeovilton on 21 August 1974, showing the flat camera nose. (*Photo: Stephen Wolf*)

Below: XJ481 again, this time a port side view with wings unfolded, showing the strange black and white colour scheme and the piping running down the tail boom. This photograph was taken at Yeovilton two years later, on 3 September 1976. (*Photo: Adrian Balch*)

Above: This Sea Vixen FAW 2, XJ494, was the last pre-production aircraft and was used by the A&AEE at Boscombe Down, for bombing technique development from April 1959 until 1962. It later joined No. 899 Squadron after conversion to Mk 2 before being assigned to Martel missile trials, initially at Hatfield in 1971, then at Boscombe Down. It was caught during these trials on finals to Boscombe Down on 13 July 1972. (*Photo: Adrian Balch*)

Number 766 Squadron's aerobatic team, 'Fred's Five' (five Sea Vixen FAW 1s plus one spare), emitting smoke and carrying varying numbers of Firestreak missiles in 1962. (*Photo: Royal Navy*)

Right: A line-up of Sea Vixen FAW 1s of No. 766 Squadron at Yeovilton on 9 July 1966, headed by XJ492. (*Photo: Adrian Balch*)

Below: This Sea Vixen FAW 1, XJ482 was withdrawn from use with No. 766 Squadron and in use by the RN Air Electric School at RNAS Lee-on-Solent, when this photograph was taken on 25 July 1970. (*Photo: Adrian Balch*)

Above: Close-up detail of No. 766 Squadron's winged-torch insignia on the fin of a Sea Vixen FAW 2 at Yeovilton on 11 March 1970. (*Photo: Adrian Balch*)

Below: A flight-line view of No. 766 Squadron Sea Vixen FAW 2s from Yeovilton's control tower on a wet 11 March 1970, with a No. 899 Squadron machine in the foreground. (*Photo: Adrian Balch*)

Above: Sea Vixen FAW 2, XN707, of No. 766 Squadron taxies in after another training sortie at Yeovilton on 11 March 1970. (*Photo: Adrian Balch*)

Right: XN685 was the second FAW 2 conversion, which first flew from Hatfield on 17 August 1962. Along with XN684, it was allocated to Red Top missile trials at Hatfield and Boscombe Down with No. 13 Joint Services Trials Unit. It then participated in trials with the Martel missile programme and is seen near Hatfield on 9 June 1970. This aircraft still survives with the Midland Air Museum at Coventry. (*Photo: Dick Winfield*)

Below: A nice flying shot of a No. 766 Squadron Sea Vixen FAW 1, XJ558, on approach to Yeovilton in September 1964. (*Photo: Werner Gysin-Aegerter collection*)

Above: Sea Vixen FAW 2, XN699, of No. 890 Squadron arrives back at Yeovilton after another training sortie on 21 August 1969. (*Photo: Adrian Balch*)

Left: Close-up detail of No. 890 Squadron's badge on the tail of a Sea Vixen FAW 2 on 11 March 1970. (*Photo: Adrian Balch*)

Above: For their final year of operation, No. 890 Squadron revised their tail badge with a white outline, as seen on FAW 2, XP919, at Yeovilton on 14 July 1971. XP919 was the first production Sea Vixen 2, which made its maiden flight from Chester on 8 March 1963. It went to Bedford for deck landing trials, flew with the full load of four Red Top missiles and completed other trials at Hatfield in 1963 and at Boscombe Down the following year. With trials complete, it finally joined No. 766 Squadron in 1968 until transfer to No. 890 Squadron in 1971. It was retired to Abingdon on 2 August 1971 for service at Halton as ground instructional airframe 8163M, but was acquired by Leisure Sport at Chertsey for preservation, who passed it on to the Norwich Air Museum on 25 August 1981. It is currently with the Blyth Valley Aviation Collection at Walpole. (*Photo: Stephen Wolf*)

Right: A close-up of the No. 890 Squadron revised tail badge on XP919 at Abingdon on 18 September 1971. (*Photo: Adrian Balch*)

Left: This Sea Vixen FAW 2, XJ524, wore the early markings of No. 892 Squadron and the 'H' denoting HMS *Hermes*, when it appeared in the static park at the Biggin Hill Air Fair on 13 May 1966. (*Photo: Author's collection*)

Left: A good deck view of No. 892 Squadron Sea Vixen FAW 2s accompanied by Buccaneers on board HMS *Hermes* in 1966. (*Photo: FAA Museum*)

Below: In February 1968, No. 892 Squadron disembarked HMS *Hermes* for RNAS Yeovilton, where Lt-Cdr Simon Idiens formed the aerobatic team, 'Simon's Sircus' with six Sea Vixen FAW 2s. Here, XN687 heads a line-up of the team's aircraft at Yeovilton on 4 September 1968. (*Photo: Adrian Balch*)

Right: A fine air-to-air shot of No. 892 Squadron 'Simon's Sircus' Sea Vixen FAW 2s overflying HMS *Hermes* in 1968. Note the centre aircraft has not had its tail badge completed. (*Photo: FAA Museum*)

Above: A publicity shot of No. 892 Squadron 'Simon's Sircus' aerobatic team practising near Yeovilton in 1968, with caricature artwork added. (*Photo: FAA Museum*)

Below: 'Simon's Sircus' in action, with six Sea Vixen FAW 2s of No. 892 Squadron trailing blue smoke, leading No. 809 Squadron's 'Phoenix Five' team of five Buccaneer S 2s during Yeovilton's Air Day on 7 September 1968. (*Photo: Adrian Balch*)

Above: Close-up detail of No. 892 Squadron 'Simon's Sircus' badge on XN687. (*Photo: Adrian Balch*)

Above: Another show is over and FAW 2, XN690, of No. 892 Squadron 'Simon's Sircus' aerobatic team lands at RNAS Brawdy on 3 August 1968, touching its tailskids on the runway. (*Photo: Jeff Peck*)

Left: When Sea Vixens weren't using the buddy-buddy refuelling technique, they could also refuel from RAF Victor tankers. Here we see Sea Vixen FAW 2, XJ584, of No. 893 Squadron accompanied by a Buccaneer S 2 of No. 801 Squadron tanking from Victor K 1A, XH590, of No. 55 Squadron, RAF over Boscombe Down on 30 August 1967. (*Photo: Brian Stainer/APN*)

Left: At the time this photograph was taken, No. 893 Squadron was embarked in HMS *Victorious*, as denoted by the 'V' on the tail of FAW 2, XP954, seen at Yeovilton on 9 September 1967. (*Photo: Adrian Balch*)

Above: Two years later No. 893 Squadron were with HMS *Hermes*, but disembarked to Yeovilton for the Air Day on 6 September 1969. Here we see XN688 accompanied by two others, getting airborne during the show. As this is written, XN688 is still extant with the DERA Fire Section at Farnborough. (*Photo: Adrian Balch*)

Right: Close-up detail of No. 893 Squadron's tail badge on FAW 2, XJ571, on 6 September 1969. (*Photo: Adrian Balch*)

Right: XJ578 of No. 893 Squadron is seen on the port bow catapult of HMS *Hermes*, about to launch, on 12 June 1968. Note the code 'last two' of the code '254' repeated on the flaps and at the rear of the right tail boom. (*Photo: Steve Hazell*)

A general view aboard HMS *Eagle* in April 1966, with Sea Vixen FAW 2s, XS577 (left) and XS584 (right) of No. 899 Squadron, accompanied by a Buccaneer S 2 and Gannet AEW 3. (*Photo: John Stevens*)

Another general carrier view, this time an earlier view aboard HMS *Ark Royal* in 1961 with Sea Vixen FAW 1s of No. 890 Squadron alongside Scimitars of No. 800 Squadron. There are Gannet AS 4s to the left and a Whirlwind HAS 7 at the rear. (*Photo: FAA Museum*)

Above: Oops, nearly lost one! This is what happens when your carrier has a list and you *think* you've got enough brake pressure to stop the aircraft moving! Sea Vixen FAW 2, XP957, of No. 899 Squadron is seen hanging precariously over the edge of HMS *Eagle*'s deck at Mombasa in December 1965. The aircraft was later winched back on board by a crane! (*Photo: John Stevens*)

Left: Seen at Yeovilton in September 1964 is FAW 2, XP958, in early No. 899 Squadron markings when based on HMS *Eagle*. Note the early black radome and the dummy yellow and blue Firestreak missiles under the wings. (*Photo: Werner Gysin-Aegerter collection*)

Above: No. 899 Squadron Sea Vixen FAW 2, XS577:133/E, about to launch from HMS *Eagle* on 7 July 1967. The Wessex HAS 1 plane guard is XS116:060/E. (*Photo: Steve Hazell*)

Right: A nice shot of XN696:123/E of No. 899 Squadron sunning itself aboard HMS *Eagle* in 1967. (*Photo: Steve Hazell*)

Above: A splendid flight deck view showing Sea Vixen FAW 2s of No. 899 Squadron, including XJ577:122/E, on board HMS *Eagle* during an exercise in the Moray Firth in July 1967. (*Photo: Steve Hazell*)

Left: A dramatic action photograph of Sea Vixen FAW 2, XN691, of No. 899 Squadron firing a salvo of rockets from two underwing Matra pods *circa* 1970. (*Photo: Royal Navy*)

Above: To prove the sun does shine at Yeovilton, Sea Vixen FAW 2, XN657: 123/E displays its No. 899 Squadron markings to effect in this port side view on 2 September 1970. As this is written, this aircraft still survives in a scrap yard at Stock, Essex. (*Photo: Adrian Balch*)

Right: End of a sortie – Sea Vixen FAW 2, XP959 of No. 899 Squadron returns to Yeovilton in 1970. (*Photo: Royal Navy*)

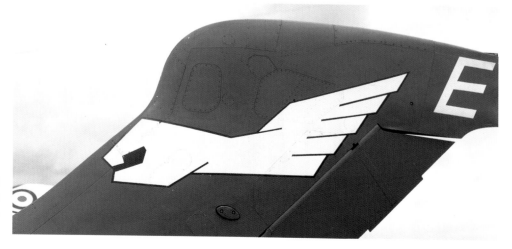

Right: A close-up of No. 899 Squadron's winged-fist insignia on XN706 at Yeovilton on 11 March 1970. (*Photo: Adrian Balch*)

Above: The last Fleet Air Arm unit to operate the Sea Vixen was the Fleet Requirements Unit, which, combined with the Airwork-managed Air Direction School, replaced its Sea Venoms at Yeovilton with Sea Vixens in January 1971. On 1 December 1972, the unit was renamed Fleet Requirements and Air Direction Unit (FRADU) and continued operating Sea Vixens until they were finally withdrawn in February 1974. Sea Vixen FAW 2, XP954:753, is seen making a low approach to Yeovilton's runway on 22 March 1972. (*Photo: Adrian Balch*)

Left: The Royal Naval Aircraft Yard at Belfast had long provided engineering support for the Sea Vixen and had retained a single example for use by the resident Maintenance Test Pilots. Over the years, they operated two aircraft, of which FAW 2, XJ572:BL, was the latter. It was withdrawn from use when the yard closed in July 1973. It is seen here at Greenham Common on 7 July 1973. (*Photo: Adrian Balch*)

Above: With their flying career over, three of the Fleet Air Arm Sea Vixens went to No. 1 School of Technical Training (SoTT) at RAF Halton in 1971 and some went to No. 2 SoTT at RAF Cosford, for apprentice ground instructional duties. Others went to the RAF College at Cranwell and some to the Royal Naval School of Aircraft Handling at Culdrose. XN691 was one of the Halton machines, had all naval markings removed and was given the maintenance serial, 8143M as seen there on 29 June 1974. (*Photo: John Hughes*)

Right: Sea Vixens for Ground Instruction. Here we see RAF Halton's three Sea Vixen FAW 2s, 8140M/XJ571, 8143M/XN691 and 8145M/XP921 on 28 September 1985, which their final year as ground instructional airframes for RAF apprentices. (*Photo: Adrian Balch*)

One of the last Sea Vixens left flying was this FAW 2, XN653, operated by the Royal Aircraft Establishment from Bedford. It didn't have the bulged observer's hatch, and had the 'Royal Navy' legend removed from the boom and an RAF fin flash added to the tail. It is seen here dramatically banking round for the photographer, on departure from Greenham Common on 2 August 1976. This clearly reveals the walkway restriction markings on top of the fuselage. (*Photo: Adrian Balch*)

This is XJ524, the first Sea Vixen FAW 2 (TT) for the aborted target-tug and drone programme, seen at Tarrant Rushton on 10 May 1978, during conversion by Flight Refuelling Ltd. (*Photo: Adrian Balch*)

The same aircraft stored at Bournemouth–Hurn on 25 January 1984, after funds ran out and the project was abandoned. The aircraft flew limited sorties from Hurn during 1979/80 in the development of a new high-speed towed-target system. Two months after this photograph was taken, this aircraft was taken to Catterick, where it was used for fire training. (*Photo: Paul Tomlin*)

Above: XS577 was one of the three completed Sea Vixen D 3 drones that was eventually delivered to RAE Llanbedr and flown in connection with the development of a Universal Drone Pack and later an Advanced Target Aircraft Control System. XS577 was active until 1990, but the following year it was withdrawn from use and used for spares to keep XP924 flying. This photograph was taken at Hurn on 18 August 1984, just after the programme had been cancelled and this aircraft was up for disposal. It was later scrapped, with the nose going to an enthusiast in Switzerland. (*Photo: Adrian Balch*)

Right: Sea Vixen D 3, XS577, seen getting airborne from Tarrant Rushton on a test flight in 1980. (*Photo: Flight Refuelling Ltd*)

Above: XS587 was the second Sea Vixen FAW 2 (TT) showing the revised colour scheme at Hurn on 19 July 1981. This aircraft undertook trials at Hurn in the early 1980s and was used at Llanbedr from at least 1983, for radio ranging trials. It was back at Hurn by August 1984 for disposal. (*Photo: Stephen Wolf*)

Right: By 1986, XS587 had been bought by Jet Heritage Ltd at Hurn, who registered it as G-VIXN in anticipation of putting it on the air show circuit. However, costs and CAA paperwork made this increasingly difficult, so it was decided to dispose of this aircraft, which went to the Gatwick Aviation Museum at Charlwood, where it resides today. (*Photo: Adrian Balch*)

Above: Further Sea Vixen FAW 2s were delivered to Flight Refuelling Ltd at Hurn for drone conversion, following their retirement from the Fleet Air Arm. However, this pair never got any further than being parked outside the hangar, once the project was cancelled. XJ602 and XN697 are seen at Hurn on 25 January 1984 still wearing their No. 893 Squadron markings from their time aboard HMS *Hermes*, awaiting their fate, which was to be scrapped! (*Photo: Paul Tomlin*)

Right: One unusual location to find a Sea Vixen was in Singapore! This is XJ490, which was an ex-899 Squadron machine, which went unserviceable while HMS *Eagle* was visiting Singapore in the late 1970s. It was too expensive to make it serviceable again, so it was donated to a fledgling museum on Sentosa Island, where it was photographed on 15 November 1986. The humid Far Eastern climate, however, took its toll on the airframe which was subsequently scrapped. (*Photo: John Mounce*)

The last surviving airworthy Sea Vixen is D 3 XP924, now registered G-CVIX with de Havilland Aviation Ltd and is currently based at Bournemouth. Here is XP924 during its heyday as an FAW 2 with No. 899 Squadron as '134/E' whilst disembarked from HMS *Eagle* to RNAS Yeovilton on 22 April 1970. It is hoped that this aircraft will be restored to this colour scheme and markings. (*Photo: Adrian Balch*)

XP924 looking in pristine condition twelve years later as a D 3 drone conversion outside Flight Refuelling's hangar at Hurn on 2 August 1982, caught just prior to being delivered to RAE Llanbedr. (*Photo: Stephen Wolf*)

XP924 is seen here arriving at Bournemouth on Bank Holiday Monday 29 May 2000 to a welcome from a crowd of enthusiasts, including former de Havilland employees from nearby Christchurch, who had worked on the Sea Vixen production line. For a history of this aircraft, see page 73. (*All photos: Adrian Balch*)

Right: Nose undercarriage leg detail on XP924/G-CVIX.

Far right: The observer's bulged hatch and window on XP924.

Below: XP924's wing-folding detail with complicated hydraulic attachments.

Twin booms meet! Close-up detail of the tail markings on XP924/G-CVIX with de Havilland Aviation Ltd's Vampire T 11, XE920/G-VMPR behind, which escorted the Sea Vixen from Swansea to Bournemouth on 29 May 2000.

Right: The pilot's cockpit of XP924, revealing 1950s technology.

Below: Another view of the cockpit, looking vertically down and showing seat detail.

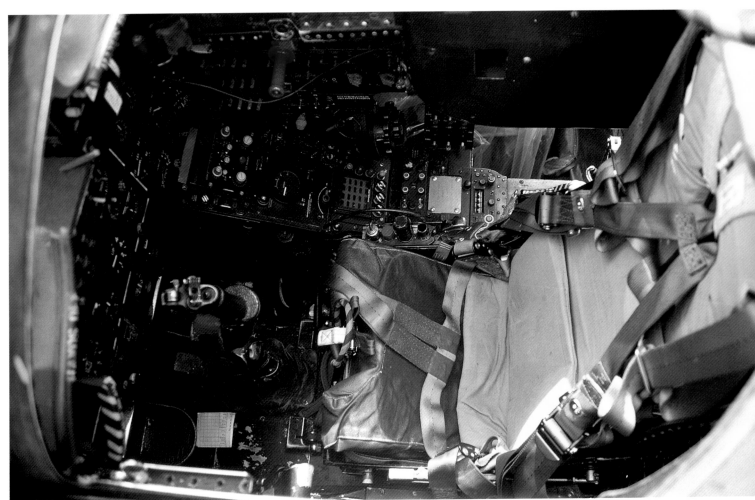

Above: XP924/G-CVIX at rest at Bournemouth on 29 May 2000, following its ferry flight from Swansea.

Right: A view looking down into the observer's open hatch – an extremely tight location – not a nice place to have to endure a long flight!

Left: Looking down the rear fuselage, this view shows all the walkway restriction markings that were applied to the top of the fuselage on all Sea Vixens.

Below: Made it at last! Pilot Sepp Pauli (left) and Clive Rustin, give happy smiles at Hurn on 29 May 2000, after having successfully flown XP924 once more, and all the hard work and waiting has finally paid off.

And finally ... so as not to disappoint all the onlookers waiting for XP924 to arrive from Swansea on 29 May 2000, a 'substitute' Sea Vixen was on hand in case it didn't make it! Just in case you were wondering, XJ571 is a real surviving Sea Vixen that is with the Brooklands Museum, following its ground instructional use at RAF Halton.

Sea Vixen survivors

FAW 1

XJ476* Southampton Hall of Aviation, Southampton, Hampshire.
XJ481 RNAY Fleetlands Museum, NARO Fleetlands, Hampshire.
XJ482 Norfolk & Suffolk Aviation Museum, Flixton, Suffolk.
XJ488* Robertsbridge Aviation Society, Robertsbridge, East Sussex.

FAW 2

XJ490 Queensland Air Museum, Caloundra, Queensland, Australia.
XJ494 Phoenix Aviation, Bruntingthorpe, Leicestershire.
XJ560 Newark Museum, Winthorpe, Nottinghamshire.
XJ565 de Havilland Heritage Centre/Mosquito Aircraft Museum, London Colney, Herts.
XJ571 Brooklands Museum, Weybridge, Surrey.
XJ575* Wellesbourne Wartime Museum, Welshbourne Mountford, Warwickshire.
XJ579* Midland Air Museum, Coventry Airport, Warwickshire.
XJ580 Tangmere Military Aviation Museum, Tangmere, West. Sussex.
XJ607* Queensland Air Museum, Caloundra, Queensland, Australia.
XN647 Flambards Village Theme Park, Helston, Cornwall.
XN650* Roy and Sue Jerman, Welshpool, Powys, Wales.
XN651* Communications & Electronics Museum, Bletchley Park, Bucks.
XN696* Blyth Valley Aviation Collection, Walpole, Suffolk.
XP919 Blyth Valley Aviation Collection, Walpole, Suffolk.
XP925* Sea Vixen Preservation Group/1268 Sqn, ATC, Haslemere, Surrey.
XP956 Privately owned, Surrey.
XS576 Imperial War Museum, Duxford, Cambridgeshire.
XS590 Fleet Air Arm Museum, RNAS Yeovilton, Somerset.

FAW 2 (TT)

XS587 Gatwick Aviation Museum, Charlwood, Surrey.

D 3

XN657* Privately owned, Yateley, Hampshire.
XP924 de Havilland Aviation, Bournemouth, Dorset.
XS577* Privately owned, Switzerland.

(* Denotes nose/cockpit section only)